NOWHERE WAS A LAKE

NOWHERE WAS A LAKE

POEMS | MARGARET DRAFT

FOUR WAY BOOKS

TRIBECA

LIBRARY OF CONGRESS CATALOGING-IN-PUBLICATION DATA
Names: Draft, Margaret, author.
Title: Nowhere was a lake : poems / Margaret Draft.
Description: New York : Four Way Books, 2024.
Identifiers: LCCN 2023031690 (print) | LCCN 2023031691 (ebook) | ISBN
    9781954245884 (trade paperback) | ISBN 9781954245891 (ebook)
Subjects: LCGFT: Poetry.
Classification: LCC PS3604.R334 N69 2024 (print) | LCC PS3604.R334
    (ebook) | DDC 811/.6--dc23/eng/20230914
LC record available at https://lccn.loc.gov/2023031690
LC ebook record available at https://lccn.loc.gov/2023031691

This book is manufactured in the United States of America and printed on acid-free paper.

Four Way Books is a not-for-profit literary press. We are grateful for the assistance
we receive from individual donors, public arts agencies, and private foundations
including the NEA, NEA Cares, Literary Arts Emergency Fund, and the
New York State Council on the Arts, a state agency.

PROUD MEMBER

[clmp]

We are a proud member of the Community of Literary Magazines and Presses.

CONTENTS

for Aaron

&

for Jacob

NOWHERE WAS A LAKE

And he told me nowhere was a lake that,
any day now, he'd surely drown in.

"Bluegrass"
Carl Phillips

Colic

He found it in the pasture,
pulse fast, pawing hay.

He stood over the still
moving body, watching it turn

in the folds of wet soil,
and after hours of contemplation,

decided to give it sleep. He waited
one more day before burying it.

What do you do when a horse dies?
You hollow out the land,

you try to make enough space,
and when you think you have enough,

keep digging.
He said this because

he himself had to enter the hole
with the horse and shovel,

shift the legs, reposition the head.

I

What Happened to James E. Tetford

Suppose Tetford stepped off the bus unnoticed at the stop before Bennington.
That he elected the woods. That he saw a darkness. That he decided to follow it.

Luminous the dark where air smells of aster in rain—why not settle
where honey swells burst, sweetening the tree's star-shaped cleft?

The bus driver, after easing into the final stop on his nightly route,
reported Tetford did not get off the bus at the stop before Bennington.

If what is real is what is witnessed, I finally know why I speak my losses
into a clear lake. Faraway footfalls. Old suitcase with a broken latch.

Suppose Tetford stepped off the bus unnoticed at the stop before Bennington.
Hoofprints that lead to a stream are covered with leaves.

Appendix

In the early evening, mice scurry back under the porch and stoke their tiny fires. Meanwhile, I am left standing wanting something imprecise latched to that sliver of light wedged between the trees.

And yet I know the layers through which the scalpel cuts. How profound the period of convalescence. How fragmented. And of fragments I have given some thought. How the kind nurse with soft hands leaning over the folds of hospital gown gathered at my thighs recited Keats—*This living hand, now warm and capable / Of earnest grasping ... in the icy silence ... haunt thy days ... red life*—I missed a few words. What happens in the end.

Today, showering, I wondered what you might say the next time you see me naked. How I might say with surprising aplomb, pointing to the fading scar on my abdomen: *each abrasion: a bloom. Absence amiss. Abandon a bridge. Addendum. Something attached.*

Mobile

If I was seeking comfort, I didn't know where to find it. I searched the fields. I peeled back the petals of a purple flower. Eventually, I found a horse at the edge of the pasture. Shifting under a partial moon. Not entirely alone or lonely. But sad like these birds constructed of paper slowly folding in on themselves.

Winter quivers under the vent. Heat on blast. All perfectly still, however, come summer. Unless I open a window. When I open a window. Inside something outside enters.

Feral

His resolve.
His division, also,
the last time they made love.

Something else gained
control. Against the cold shower wall,
it thrust itself.

She was unable to identify
what it looked like, the end
the first time there was one.

It put a cup of dirt in her hands.
No more, no less.
It wanted to see what she would do with it,

if she would flinch.
She was afraid to show it she would.
She was afraid to show it she wouldn't.

II

On the Disappearance of Paula Jean Welden

My cousin Donald tells me the story slowly, knowing I'm the kind of person
who excites over unsolved, unresolved things.

He tells me my grandfather believed this girl just wanted to be forgotten

or that she fell into one of the old mines behind the barns in which,
one season, he lost two cows.

It wasn't a huge loss.

Of course, no one ever did check the mines.

Not even my grandfather.

Even now, I can picture him leaning hard against his truck, thinking
of the girl while watching my mother drift in the windblown grass.

She Didn't Want Another Child

Fall of 1953, Jean fell down the stairs, barreled
into the living room into a heated game of *go fish*.

She fell because she didn't want another tractor,
she didn't want another boy to work on the farm,

another boy to trample on
rhubarb or rhododendron.

Elbows dusted with baby powder,
only stirring when the leaves shook

on the elm outside the east window,
she wanted more time to think about swimming,

applying sunscreen to the back of her neck
knowing, not caring, she will burn either way,

drowning in the light of late summer,
drifting to the image of seagulls lining the dock.

Fledgling

1

I stand at the window and look in. I watch my desire, the urgency of it, expand and lessen.

2

You are inside the house.

I want to touch your hand.

3

When my mother tells me that, when she thinks of the first person she loved, the boy with whom she spent a whole summer in a tepee fifty years ago, she still pictures him as a seventeen-year-old.

4

These long-
suffering
and affectionate shadows.

I think I understand what this means.

5

When I ask my mother if she is also seventeen when she thinks of that summer, she says she cannot see herself.

June Thoughts

Pantry stuffed with mustards and oils, tomatoes in terracotta pots—
you said once I think only in kitchens

and I suspect you're right, also that you're still tall and thin,
walking with a cold drink to the beach, thinking of me once or twice.

In this town, wheat flexes in the fields.
Cows extend their necks to the sky.

If you wrote, I might tell you I still drive by Ide Road,
roll down the window, peek through the trees

hoping to catch a glimpse of someone pass
through the breezeway, a chimera, a boy

teaching a younger version of myself how to breathe
after a nightmare, palm pressed hard against my chest.

I wonder what you do in California.
It is my dream, I suppose, that you are planting lemon trees.

To the Stars on the Wings of a Pig

It is written somewhere in the sky—we are supposed to forget quickly. How? An elephant stands on a tiny pedestal. In a field under a tent. The ringmaster spectacular in his tails and topcoat, expert in redirection, points towards the acrobat. The acrobat astounds because he *could* fall.

The other day I told my friend the story in which you fell through the floorboards of an old barn. As I told the story, I recalled the manner in which you carefully transferred milk to a newborn calf. You beckoned to Babette singing *come Bossy Boss come Boss.*

Years since you carved onto your forearm that pig with wings, but have you ever noticed that the word *pigeon* contains the word *pig*? Once, in the evening on Fifth or Third, I saw a pigeon plummet into a vat of mustard. I watched its dark wings thrash. Then yield.

Floriography

Moved by the familiar unmarked page. Victorian herbarium. Docents shuffling up and down the stairs. Do I have to justify using the word *pianoforte* in a poem when I know it will not likely serve a greater purpose? I suppose I reserve the right to decide either way. To preserve exotic flora between the pages of my twenties. Men without fathers. Pressed marsh marigold and anemone. Let me first open the museum before I tell you what lies on the other side of this sentence. August. Enamored of the poet I only imagined kissing in Emily's garden. Daffodil or phlox. In the end, I unearthed that he was both and neither.

Unsent Letter #6

What choice did I have?

To bury or to burrow.
To fear
or to fare.

If nothing else,
I learned how to hold
desire in my body
so long
my chest bloomed
into a meadow
of violets.

I Can't See the Forest for the Trees

Today, in the glove compartment of my car,
I found the faded
peony petal you placed there
last summer beside a row of pennies.

You exist.
You exist less.

What are you doing on the other side of this door?
Steeping tea, plum in mouth?
Drawing a bath?

I never liked the prepositional *moving on*.
To where?
From what?

I keep coming back to this
sad stoop.
To these smaller
monuments, lesser
known as they are.

Your hand there.
My hand here.
Your hand nearer.
Nearer.

Elegy for the Elusive Ivory-Billed Woodpecker

Once was the poet from Kansas
kindly cautioning—

this is a sad and beautiful book—

what he inscribed
in the only one he'd give to me.

Truth be told, I don't know what became of him.

But some nights I still think to reach
my hand into the void.

To write something tender.

To address him as Lord God.

Lord God, I forgive you for seeming gone.
Lord God, someone saw you in Highlands County, Florida.

Interrogating the Ghost

When I have a fever,
do you move into the living room?
Do you simply walk through one wall
and then another?
Do you know what those white flowers are,
the flowers in our yard?
Would you call me cowardly?
Would you move to Utah if I said you had to?
Did you see the coyote I saw,
the one Aaron says was a dog?
Do you feel that passing
moment of resignation
when I fix my gaze on a wall
on a hole where a nail used to be?
Are you uncomfortable when we make love?
Do you shift behind the dresser
and watch until the very end
when I am lying next to him
when I say good enough
and when I mean exactly that?
This is good *and* enough.
This life. This house.
These walls.
I don't know what to call them,
those white flowers.

Mouse in the Cardboard Box

For levity, we called it a hotel, one for which I left a promising review:
modest accommodations—newspaper and wool—but hard to object

to the complimentary banana slice and flexible cancellation policy,
should you wish to check out sooner. Should you wish to.

Out of the cat's mouth. Out from under the portable pump organ.
I can't say how many days it's been since we moved you to the end

of our driveway, if you remained in the box and there remain still.
I should have mentioned the window. Carved into the box, a small hole

overlooks a field extending northward somewhere, a warm corner
in a cowshed or stable. A hole just large enough to escape out of.

Postmortem

When I turn towards you in the morning,
and when you rest a forgiving
hand on my shoulder,
I begin to believe there is a life raft at the end of this story.

Except there is no end.
No life raft.
Only the rope you might throw
compassionately in my direction.

Nothing will change,
I want to say,
knowing this is a lie.
Knowing you also know this is a lie.

I don't know what lies on the other side of this paradigm.
An anxious fawn?
Leaping out of
and back into that untenable garden.

Thank you for making the bed.
For these unspoken
transmissions. I don't need to tell you
I'm still holding a shadow in my fist.

Your Lips Taste Like Someone Else

Even though my husband agreed to this,
I don't know why I'm still policing

the pathway, searching
for someone who might know me.

You: promiscuous.
You: adulteress.

Ungrateful strayer.
Greedy slut.

When you take a picture of me with your phone,
I take an imaginary one of you with my hands.

The Angler

You cast your line, unlike mine,
assertively over the Swift River.

This is not so different:
what you and I do, who you and I are.

Your lure.
This possible poem.

This is where my mind lately travels.
Late at night. In the dark.

In parallel solitude.
In quiet estuaries.

With me, you downstream
drift and drag.

But when you wade
with delayed

gratification, my kind of spectator
sport, my arousal—

our distance still:
still our distance:

a fly in the throat,
stuck, or choosing to be stuck,

bobbing in the middle of this,
some nameless current

you invited me to—
self-consciously, together

I string a series of meaningless words.
You tie an elaborate knot.

Limerence

outside

two birds

shyly

court

one another

one   is slightly

more

in pursuit

of the other

how unfortunate

this is all

I seem to observe

Where There Are Tracks, There Are Also Beds

When you grab my hand and guide me
to the half-made bed in the woodshed apartment

I only half-furnished, I am already hoof-to-hoof.
Scotch-tipsy and collared.

Tug on the leash and I'll comply.
But I have nothing of substantial value to offer you.

This starved body for a night. This appetite.
Once whet, spoiled.

Hemlocks sentinel these subtle depressions.
This is where deer bed, you said, hours earlier,

pointing to the snow's soft edges,
last night holding the lone doe's spine.

When you go home tonight—back to your apartment,
back to your partner—there will be shot

glasses in the sink to rinse.
A set of snowshoe imprints

moving away from the woodshed.
I don't know how to explain the enormity

and inconsequence of these already
fading tracks. I don't want to wash the sheets.

Dear Metamour

When he arrives a minute after midnight,
smelling of me, musk & honey,
and if he seems different or indifferent,
distant or distracted,
and if he's not fighting you over the Roku,
and if, in bed, he has his back to you,
and if he doesn't see you staring absently
at the ceiling, or, worse, the floor,
tears welling, supposing you'll soon sleep
in separate beds or separate
rooms or simply decide to separate,
please, know I have also slept alone
in the same remote home with my husband.
He returns every week. Every week, he returns
slowly, limb by limb. And I, too,
pace those same dimly lit corridors.
That I am boring and dispensable.
Once luminous, now moonless.

When a Dog Runs

laps around the pond, it is also running around
the lapping ripples my feet make
in the shape of an unanswerable question.

Pondering
each circle inside another:
smaller, larger, intersecting.

You and me.
You and her.
You and him.
Them and them.
Then them.
Then then.

I wish I were a dog.
I wish I had never
become a dog.

Running breathless
laps around the pond.
Then barking at my own reflection.

Edge

Most nights, I close my fist
tightly, as if to grasp
not what I can't keep
but what won't keep me.

His hands firmly
around my throat.

This is one way to say I have control.
This is one way to say I have you.

The dialectic of trust.

It is not a question of whether you will
harm me, but whether you will
stick around long enough
to hold me when I am harmed.

Purgatory
is a safe place in the woodshed.

There are safewords.

But not safe people in it.

A Disturbance

Of the many things
we wished to forget,
belonging mostly to that
reckless consort,
some days foaming
at the mouth, others
cautiously backed
into the corner of its cage,
we each chose one stone,
one thing to let go of,
consigned to us
by someone else,
to cast into the river.

Of the many things
we wished to forget,
and of the one thing
we each chose,
what I remember
most is not what I wished
to forget, or the shape
of the stone I picked,
but the stillness of the river.
That we forgot
what we came to forget.
Then broke the stillness
with our stones.

The Doe

Feasting on a small blade of grass.

Sensing something else
breathing in the shadows,
she stops.

She sees,
what does she see,
or not see, that I recognize,
or try to, in her, also?

June came and went.

When you said you didn't know if you should go,
what stopped me from telling you to stay?

Sometimes phantoms leave the body quickly.
Sometimes they never leave at all.

I wonder when I will finally step into myself.
What will be the cause of that?
Who?
Isn't the question always who?

Sated,
or so it seems,
the doe slowly
steps back into the forest.

III

Finding the Woodsman

At the end of the road, a doe
dead under a sign: *Dead End*.

After all these years,
I'm still turning
every stone, looking
under every hoof.

To find a stream.
A rifle cartridge.
An ankle
poking through the dirt like a tulip.

Rebound

A dense fog lifts.
Then another.

July dahlias.
Obedience.
Breaches
of trust.

Late bloomers
fall out of favor.

Who's faster, off
to greener pastures?

Dead things
flourish underwater.
Bewildered.

Just out of reach—
yesterday's blossoms.

Now that you are gone,
from my palm
taste this
sweet
bleeding blackberry.

Story About a Body

you're so beautiful so thin said the last one the first time she undressed
herself in front of him

at which point she shrugged *just as well I'm already lost*

and how small she'd become so small no one who knew her knew
where to look for her anymore

that double sawing illusion what a marvelous trick a woman cut in half

no applause
no audience

only the animals they dared to look when she slammed her head

against the steering wheel in the middle of a plowed field she plowed
her car into wondering *why am I here who for*

The Campbells Will Always Sleep
at the Red Roof Inn

What now, if nothing else? If nothing more?

I need nothing more.

Nothing more is nomadic.
Nothing more is a bull in a china shop.
Nothing more is gentle.

Let me not taint more with more. Let me not be greedy, having held more.
More poems & prose. More sweat & expletives. More God. Your head
tipped back, screaming at a merciful, however unremarkable, sky, *God, I'm
good, I'm a good person, I swear*, though wanting more. A stranger in a bar.
A bruised peach, more. The horseshoe bend in the river.

Who do you think you are?
A flash in the pan.
A flask of scotch.
We adopt alternative personas.

Vivian pins Clint's arms down in the grass.
Vivian wants to tell Clint she's nervous.
Vivian wants Clint to lie down again.

She also wants back-to-back sidewalk dancing & western ballads. She also
wants more. And who can blame her? More scotch & citrus. More cheap
motels. Innocent & illicit. She wants to watch this stranger, her husband
for a single night, slip into a deep sleep. She wants to gently touch his
gentle face. Room 158. Not an abandoned warehouse. Not a train car.

Home sweet home is homeless. Home sweet home is somewhere. Home sweet home is anywhere, nowhere.

God, pray, she can hold herself together in the car. God, pray, she can see him, once more, looking at her, driving out of the parking lot. Hitching west to live with nothing on his back. God, pray, she can sit back & watch. God, pray, she can also be good. That she can live with nothing more. One more hour. One night more. One more round of Johnnie Walker. More burn & blunder. No thing: forever. The impression their bodies made in the grass late the night before. Here they were. Here we are. Look at all the crushed clover.

Hand Me That American Spirit

Because you can never canter
back whence you came,
coming over the tracks, soiling
the rails—

or so I have been told—

but I have been told so many things,

so many half-truths.

How horses, decades dead, are neighing in the pasture.

How strangers lock eyes in a bar every hour,
but rarely are both people changed by this.

Headway

Because I have known safety
from the pulpit.

Because, to measure the water's
depth, you must measure it
fathom by fathom.

Darker, further.
Pull on the halyard.

Because I only get one life.

I will lower
and hoist
my own sails.

Plain Meeting House Cemetery
in West Greenwich, Rhode Island

Both the dead and the living. She is straddling
him in the graveyard, his back pressed against a grave.

Where did they go when they wanted to go
or thought to go wherever they went together to go?

She takes off, dancing across
the dirt path, and he follows.

They pretend they don't know what the other person wants.
They are resting under the gentle boughs of never knowing.

She kisses his throat. He swallows.
The ants crawl beneath his back.

Under her dress: an eternity.
Between her legs, he reaches for it.

She wants to be someone else just this once.
Someone, even if no one in particular, to him.

Next to them:
a quiet church.

What does it matter if no one or someone
saw them laying in the grass?

She thinks, gazing at him, here is a grave.
Here are my hands.

Let me pray now with your mouth.
Let me run my fingers slowly through your hair.

Plums Out of Your Palms

oh

       lavender

summer you do

do you
not with this

       autumn advancing

       bursting
       bouquet

hear me singing

auburns
summer sweetly

listening to your injured

       resilient

not yet to tell

             i called
             and called

the thought silently
dawning
but faithful

i have been calling it
by a different
name

all these desperately

                 solitary
          but accompanied
          years

                      under another

       felled

                 and heavy
                 deciduous

i'm only as good
as the next
felled

one to come along
i think

                but prey

or dead

forest-
ensnared

                singing
now that i have heard you
                singing

      my hands
      are as good as tied

Purview

On the one hand, I cannot unsee the things I saw.
On the other, I cannot see the things I saw in the same way again.

That was then.

For the time being, I have seen all that I possibly can.

I can see that now.

Laying Her Upon the Bale

startled

the pigeons

what are these
    things
    groping

in the dark
what they do
what they never seem to
finish

beneath the rafters
is

        brome
        matted

pushing
        and pulling

each coarse

strand

hay   from

hair

                                        inside her

how many women have laid here

how many women have fallen
off a bale
and laughed

        loft

                                        dust

        filling   their lungs

Traveling through the Dark Again

Think only thoughts of glaciers and salt flats.
Not another poem about a poem about a fawn never to be born.

Every incident before.
Every swerving.

The open canyon.

Oh, had we swerved
a moment sooner or later: another fatality.

But you do not yet know how much I grieve a thing still breathing.
That I'm pushing it, never once to use its legs, over the ledge.

Lucid Dreams & Small Nightmares

1

Every object in the room,
plenty and too much.

Made to be unmade.

Even the bed.
Especially the bed.

2

Biting my lip, what if I stop biting it?
What happens then?

You're dreaming,
light-deeply
to some alarming
locale.

3

Hiding in the grass amongst the insects, Nomad of the small & lawless.
Nomad Boxcar. Nomad made it to Buffalo. He got drunk. Catching
out, Nomad could have died. No One on tomorrow's beaten trestles.
Misstepping. Dreaming of a softer breeze.

4

Let me tell you a short story about a man who came to me in the middle
of the night.

He walked across a bed of moss beneath the conifers and spoke
until he couldn't.

Tongue-tied.
Orange slices outstretched
in his palms.

5

How long does this go on?

Dead-end
questions are just that,
a candle
burning at both ends.

How many men have fallen in love with my candles?
How many men have fallen
in love with me falling in love with them
or the stories I tell them about the men
I have fallen in love with?

6

How little I know and about so much.

A little flour in the pantry.
A little less.
A little wildflower.
A little wild.
Blue aster.

7

How little I know about you and about so much.
How you sleep.

Moan
or yell.

8

All love is,
not waking
your light-deeply
sleeping lover
from good dreams
or bad ones
with your candles.

A Little Wild

When he recited her poem
by the bay, she could tell
he was nervous.

He'd stumble
over a word.
Then repeat it.

Like her,
he wanted to get it
just right.

But now that he is not nervous,
she is the one stumbling
over the steps of an abandoned church.

No One Steps in the Same River Twice

Thank you, Heraclitus.

But maybe it's reasonable to try.

To wet the cuffs
of your jeans
in the same stream
and say

Yes, this is how
I remember it.

Backing away,
you repeated
my name.

How many times did you repeat it?
Five? Six?
Who does that?

What returns
returns the same,
though I never feel
the same way about it.

One night, gone
stag.

One night, gone
home.

One night, home
gone.

I don't know how anyone
does anything
walking backwards.

Hearth

Staring at the fire.

Then embers.

Animals war in the walls
while something small
and insidious
rots beneath us.

An incomplete thought.

On your chest,
my head: it is already cold.

Self-doubt
begets self-doubt.

A body trembling,
requesting affirmation,
then, in the absence of one,
turns away slowly.

It comes as no surprise to me anymore.

That sadness almost always gives way to lust.
That lust almost always gives way again to sadness.

I'm not sure what I mean by this.

Only that all the closing
doors are hopelessly swollen.

All the missed opportunities.
Botched apologies.
Letters rarely dispatched.
Nuptials and the breaking of those.

That I gather every breaking
in my arms
like broken branches.

That I lay the broken
branches on the ashes.

I can't yet call the branches broken,
even the broken ones.

But what would I not break for you?

Dissection: Field Vole from the Foothills of Ovando

For an hour, I worked at that

      little

          pellet.

I like to think I was delicate.

      But there was so much
      matted
      fur, I crushed

          the mandible

      with my

          fingers.

he has loved. Lately, you think to yourself
I would like to be one of those women,
another carved into the skin of him.
But he's already swinging himself up
onto the next passing train. Even though
he is sleeping in your bed. Even though
he is sleeping in your bed, snoring and
talking in his sleep. *Be a dear and fetch*
me a glass of water. How lucky to
be opaque. Even when he refers to
you as his wife, you disappear in that
empty space. There is a stranger in your
bed. Listen. There is a stranger in your
bed and you already have a husband.

Fidelity

1

I stayed in the city where no one can afford a house.
I made a vow.
I spoke of the person I wanted to become.

Then I became someone else.

2

On the nightstand,
a diamond
does not sparkle in a box.

3

What can I say that you don't already know?

I have outstayed
my welcome.

And still I have not left.

Little Prayers

Here's to you, lonesome dove, gone lightly
and not yet, or too soon, and never, albeit
always. Still, I kissed the bark of the ancient
oak you told me to kiss and made a wish.
What a waste of a wish. To wish for all that
I already have. And now that I am making
the same simple and selfish wish, day in and
day out, I am in my head—typing this—
while you are, in the other room, reading.

Bow Saw

Seated on the stump with a cold Stella,
you offer only a few words of guidance.

Don't put too much weight into it.
Don't think so much.
Just draw the blade gently forward and back.

After this, you are silent.

> Watch me hardly
> saw through
> any hesitation.

> Partial things to say.

I don't know why I try so hard sometimes.

It is difficult to cut a straight line.

Laceration

All thanks to a *Risky Business* socked slide across the slick kitchen floor.

At the very least, she made one of the nurses in the ER almost piss her pants from laughter.

*

Who doesn't want to feel incandescent?

The girl laid a lifetime under the overhead fluorescent.

*

A gurney glides down the hall.

When she returned home, she adjusted her eyes to the darkened room. She was waiting for her lover, the only person who has sucked tears and blood off her fingers, to surprise her. To walk through the door before the sun rose and kiss the corner of her sutures.

*

This event never happened.

Apart from falling. She really did fall. She broke open her chin dancing by herself in the kitchen. Then, bleeding, swayed like a drunk over the vanity.

*

So much red.

Hell, I look gorgeous, red.

*

She doesn't know how long the healing will take.
When the swelling
will stop or bruises fade.

Mostly, she is concerned
she will involuntarily
touch herself and break
open one of the sutures.

She imagines telling her lover this.
That her injuries
are predominantly
self-inflicted.

Poor sweet girl,
he'll say, lightly
touching the stitches.

It is only
a small frown.

A capsized canoe.

Heel Striking the Harvest

He grabs my hand, the same one someone else
released coldly only the night before, and holds it gently.

I'm on the verge of falling apart in the face of such kindness.
Most days, I don't feel I deserve his tenderness.

Tenderness always stops
me midsentence.

Deserve? He asks. What do you mean by this?
I'm not sure anyone deserves anything they never will have, have had,

or have since lost. Long lost. My hands reaching
everyplace and anyplace for any hand but his to feel reached.

Even now, he is holding me at my worst.
Barren fields extending gradually into nothing.

In no place, going someplace, I know.
There are so few things I can say I know definitively.

But this must be the definition of plenty.
The sun slowly setting over the valley.

The darkening field: my husband—his hand
in mine, for the time being—walking me through it.

Two Tracks

Hesitating at the railyard,
he surprises himself,

choosing instead
the westbound train,

and in not choosing
the other one,

can't sleep,
can't see

outside the walls of
his own freight

car, sprawling
fields of startled

deer miles behind him
and long stretches

of prairie receding.
The other choice

rested at a pivotal
intersection,

he thinks. The split,
two tracks,

without fail,
diverge.

He knows the other
one leads

back to her.
But, from there, where?

He closes his eyes.
He forgives himself

for surprising himself.
He forgives himself

knowing she will
forgive him also.

Back pressed
against the hard

floor of his container,
he drifts off

thinking of her,
lying on a soft

mattress, his body
lunging forward.

NOTES

"What Happened to James E. Tetford," "On the Disappearance of Paula Jean Welden," and "Finding the Woodsman" are three poems loosely based on the reported disappearances of James E. Tetford, Paula Jean Welden, and Middie Rivers, three individuals who mysteriously went missing in the southwest corner of Vermont in the 1940s.

"Fledgling" borrows "These long-suffering and affectionate shadows" from "Lightning Bugs Asleep in the Afternoon" by James Wright.

"Traveling through the Dark Again" dialogues with William Stafford's "Traveling through the Dark."

ACKNOWLEDGMENTS

Sincerest thanks to the editors of the following publications in which a few of these poems first appeared, in earlier forms, or were later featured: *Poetry Daily*, *Radar Poetry*, and *Southern Humanities Review*.

Heaps of gratitude—

To the friends, mentors, institutions, and programs that supported me and my writing, including the Emily Dickinson Museum, The Frost Place, Francis W. Parker School, Smith College, and the MFA Program for Writers at Warren Wilson College, especially: Debra Allbery, Theresa Collins, Francine Conley, Maudelle Driskell, Noah Friedman, Jennifer Funk, Diana Gordon, Sarah Halper, Maya Janson, Rodney Jones, Jill Klein, Kimberly Kruge, Joan Larkin, James Longenbach, Leigh Lucas, Kate Murr, Douglas Lane Patey, Patrick Phillips, Katherine Rooks, Bonnie Seebold, Alan Shapiro, Daniel Tobin, Ellen Bryant Voigt, Connie Voisine, Ellen Doré Watson, and Ross White.

To Hannah Matheson, for your eyes on this book and editorial genius. To Ryan Murphy, for agreeing to publish it. And to Martha Rhodes, for believing in it in the first instance.

To my family, for every loving nudge and roof above: Elvy, Howard and Caroline, Andrew and Cristina, Anna and Peter, David and Glenda, Paul, Sheila, Jonathan and Jenna, Jared and Tina, Jeff and Dianna, Elsie and Piper, and Margaret and Donald.

To all the bosom buddies, confidants, and meteors over the years, for seeing me when you did and for your continued influence: Brendan Allen, Patricia Allen, Bianca Beam, Vera Beauvais, Erin Cleary, Alex Connors, Reed Dunkle, Carrie Evans, Julia Franz, Jocelyn Glaze, John

Goodhue, Tom Harper, Caitlin Hoess, Anna Holley, Jennifer Kaplan, Arielle Kirven, Celia Kokoris, Maggie Kraus, Lauren Lankhof, Elise Lasko, Allie Lopez, Dylan Makowski, Laura Malecky, Em Peake, Lisbet Portman, Katarina Nešković, Roberto Rodriguez, Joseph Rogers, Tommy Rosenbluth, Bobbie Schuster, Colin Seger, Melody Setoodehnia, Anna Vilner, Chris Willmott, and Hannah Young.

To Aaron Borucki, for having held me and the content of this collection with heroic tenderness.

And to Jacob, for being ever stalwart.

Margaret Draft is a poet based in Bennington, Vermont. She holds an AB in English Language & Literature from Smith College, where she was awarded The Ethel Olin Corbin Prize, and an MFA in Creative Writing from the Program for Writers at Warren Wilson College. She has worked at The Emily Dickinson Museum as a House Manager and The Frost Place as a Work Fellow for their Conference on Poetry. Her poems have appeared in *Radar Poetry, Southern Humanities Review*, and on *Poetry Daily*. This is her debut collection of poetry.

SELF-PORTRAIT

PUBLICATION OF THIS BOOK WAS MADE POSSIBLE
BY GRANTS AND DONATIONS. WE ARE ALSO GRATEFUL
TO THOSE INDIVIDUALS WHO PARTICIPATED IN
OUR BUILD A BOOK PROGRAM. THEY ARE:

Anonymous (14), Robert Abrams, Michael Ansara, Kathy Aponick, Jean Ball, Sally Ball, Clayre Benzadon, Adrian Blevins, Laurel Blossom, Adam Bohannon, Betsy Bonner, Patricia Bottomley, Lee Briccetti, Joel Brouwer, Susan Buttenwieser, Anthony Cappo, Paul and Brandy Carlson, Dan Clarke, Mark Conway, Elinor Cramer, Kwame Dawes, Michael Anna de Armas, John Del Peschio, Brian Komei Dempster, Rosalynde Vas Dias, Patrick Donnelly, Lynn Emanuel, Blas Falconer, Jennifer Franklin, John Gallaher, Reginald Gibbons, Rebecca Kaiser Gibson, Dorothy Tapper Goldman, Julia Guez, Naomi Guttman and Jonathan Mead, Forrest Hamer, Luke Hankins, Yona Harvey, KT Herr, Karen Hildebrand, Carlie Hoffman, Glenna Horton, Thomas and Autumn Howard, Catherine Hoyser, Elizabeth Jackson, Linda Susan Jackson, Jessica Jacobs and Nickole Brown, Lee Jenkins, Elizabeth Kanell, Nancy Kassell, Maeve Kinkead, Victoria Korth, Brett Lauer and Gretchen Scott, Howard Levy, Owen Lewis and Susan Ennis, Margaree Little, Sara London and Dean Albarelli, Tariq Luthun, Myra Malkin, Louise Mathias, Victoria McCoy, Lupe Mendez, Michael and Nancy Murphy, Kimberly Nunes, Susan Okie and Walter Weiss, Cathy McArthur Palermo, Veronica Patterson, Jill Pearlman, Marcia and Chris Pelletiere, Sam Perkins, Susan Peters and Morgan Driscoll, Maya Pindyck, Megan Pinto, Kevin Prufer, Martha Rhodes and Jean Brunel, Paula Rhodes, Louise Riemer, Peter and Jill Schireson, Rob Schlegel, Yoana Setzer, Soraya Shalforoosh, Mary Slechta, Diane Souvaine, Barbara Spark, Catherine Stearns, Jacob Strautmann, Yerra Sugarman, Arthur Sze and Carol Moldaw, Marjorie and Lew Tesser, Dorothy Thomas, Rushi Vyas, Martha Webster and Robert Fuentes, Rachel Weintraub and Allston James, Abby Wender and Rohan Weerasinghe, and Monica Youn.